Facing Death

Facing Death

Stories of Spiritual Response to Serious Illness

John H. Chapman, M.D.

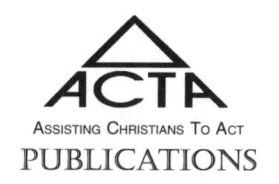

ACTA
ASSISTING CHRISTIANS TO ACT
PUBLICATIONS

Facing Death
Stories of Spiritual Response to Serious Illness
by John H. Chapman, M.D.

All the stories in this book are true and are used with permission, although names and circumstances have been changed to protect people's privacy.

Edited by Gregory F. Augustine Pierce
Cover Design by Tom A. Wright
Typesetting by Garrison Publications

Copyright ©1998 by John H. Chapman, M.D.

Published by ACTA Publications
Assisting Christians To Act
4848 N. Clark Street
Chicago, IL 60640
800-397-2282

All rights reserved. No part of this publication may be reproduced or transmitted in any form or by any means, electronic or mechanical, including photocopying and recording, or by any information storage and retrieval system, without permission from the publisher.

Library of Congress Catalog number: 97-77690
ISBN: 0-87946-177-2
Printed in the United States of America
02 01 00 99 98 5 4 3 2 1 First Printing

CONTENTS

Introduction/11

My Own Illness/15

Stephen's Family/25

David/27

Janet/33

Megan and Grandpa/37

Warren's Store/41

Donald and Chappy/45

Chappy's Death/47

Lawrence/51

Daniel/55

Anna and Peter/59

Two Funerals/63

Martha/65

Kim/69

Michael and Emily/73

Gary and Jeanean/77

Veronica/83

William/85

Helen/89

Phillip and Rose/91

Sarah/97

Harold and Ellen/101

Afterword/107

About the Author/109

To my wife, Molly, whose
strength, courage, love, and devotion
have inspired me always to be
the most that I can be.

And which of you by being anxious can add a cubit to his span of life?
Luke 12:25

The most fortunate of us, in our journey through life, frequently meet with calamities and misfortunes which may greatly afflict us, and to fortify our minds against the attacks of these calamities and misfortunes should be one of the principal studies and endeavors of our lives. The only method of doing this is to assure a perfect resignation to the Divine Will, to consider that whatever does happen, must happen; and that, by our uneasiness, we cannot prevent the blow before it does fall, but we may add to its force after it has fallen.
Thomas Jefferson

INTRODUCTION

The true stories in this collection started out as entries in a personal journal. They are about sick patients and their loved ones, often facing death but hiding in the shadow of fear. As in any diary, though, the narratives are also about me. They reveal my reactions and emotions as I came to know, care for, and learn from each individual.

I am a physician, proud of what I do and the way that I do it. I have concerns about some of the directions taken in the profession of medicine over the last twenty years, yet despite those questions I love being a doctor. I consider it the greatest privilege any man or woman could ever hope for. Many of the stories of spiritual response to serious illness in this book have to do with my vocation as a doctor.

I could not do what I do without faith in God. I am a Christian by birth and by breeding, worshipping now in a Presbyterian church. Though I struggle with uncertainties and doubts regarding theology, I have an unshakable inner strength that derives from this faith. I am convinced that healing requires a measure of spirituality and that over the years I have helped more individuals in this manner than I have with pills or procedures.

I am also a patient with a chronic illness, epilepsy. I have learned the hard way that fear is the real enemy—that by letting go of this fear and giving it to God, I am no longer a prisoner to my disease. I accept my illness. I do what I can do for it by taking my medication, but I am rid of all the rest. I live with my illness and am thankful for today.

This book is not about death. It is about facing death and living with disease. Since my field is cardiology, most of the patients included here do have heart trouble of one sort or another, but I believe that their stories are universal in their insight.

My goal is to describe the reactions of patients, families, and their doctors to chronic illness. I have chosen, therefore, to keep the medical terminology extremely basic. Heart patients get chest pain (angina); shortness of breath due to fluid in their lungs (congestive heart failure); palpitations (irregularities of the heart rhythm); heart attacks (myocardial infarctions); and, if their heart muscle is severely damaged, they may go into shock (low blood pressure), which is nearly always fatal.

Doctors cannot cure heart disease, but heart surgery (to replace a damaged valve or bypass a blocked artery, for example) can relieve symptoms and improve the quality of life for many patients. In order to consider such an option, doctors must do a test (cardiac catheterization) in which they pass a tiny tube (catheter) up into the heart to measure pressures within the various heart chambers and inject dye which enables them to take pictures of the abnormal anatomy. In some cases, doctors can actually open up blocked arteries using a catheter with a tiny balloon attached to its end (angioplasty).

There are risks involved with all of these interventions. The patient can develop complications such as heart attack, stroke, or even death. These risks must be weighed against the potential benefit in every individual case. All of the procedures have limitations; the decisions are never easy. I know, because I have to make them every day. I live with the risk because for every life lost there are twenty lives improved.

Patients facing serious illness and death must learn to cope with fear. This book is about fear, written by someone who has known it. But it is also about the need for God in the practice of medicine and about the great gift called "letting go" that is, in fact, the leap of faith.

I ask that you consider each separate narrative as a broken piece of glass. Once all the pieces are read and put together, there is a whole that emerges, creating a mirror. In this mirror you will find an image—a refracted reflection of yourself. If you look closely, you will also find God.

ONE

MY OWN ILLNESS

There is a part of this story that I don't remember, a blank space filled in by others, a few hours never registered because my mind was jumbled in an electrical distortion we medical professionals call a seizure.

My life, along with that of my wife and children, changed forever that day in ways I am only now—years later—beginning to comprehend.

The seizure was precipitated by a series of stressful circumstances. I had been invited to give an academic presentation on the subject of cardiogenic (caused by a disorder of the heart) shock at a gathering of emergency room physicians from around the state. I had prepared a good talk, put new slides together, arranged them, rehearsed, rearranged the slides, and rehearsed again. On call the night before, I did not get to bed until 2:00 a.m. In order to be ready for my ride at 5:00 A.M., I set the alarm for 4:00, giving me only two hours for a fitful pretense of sleep. When one is young and healthy, he or she does not pay attention to the dangers of something as common as sleep deprivation. After all, in my work my sleep is frequently interrupted. By itself then, this was certainly a factor but not something new.

Public speaking is for many, including myself, a major stress. I have always been intensely anxious prior to any lecture or presentation—my false confidence belied by the tremor in my hand as I direct the lighted pointer toward a darkened screen. I remember all too vividly childhood moments of inadequacy and shame, and I realize the powerful influence these moments must have had on my reaction to performance before an audience as an adult. In small groups of people whom I know, there is no such fear. I am able to teach, perform, and play sports quite capably. But the larger the audience, the smaller my ego. Confidence wanes, muscles tense, concentration wanders; my thoughts become clouded with fears of failure.

The presentation preceding mine was by a trauma surgeon. It consisted of a long series of horrible accident injuries, chosen for their explicit depiction of torn limbs, broken bodies, bloody formless masses of flesh proudly displayed as one might a collection of stamps. I have always been weak in the stomach when it comes to this gruesome aspect of medicine, and before long I felt waves of nausea and a sensation of lightheadedness coming over me—so much so that I wanted to excuse myself. But it was too late.

The lights came on and, seemingly without warning, I was being introduced as the next speaker. My fate was sealed.

Long before any true symptoms occurred, my mind was racing, aware of some impending danger, sensing calamity but not cognizant of the villain. I was losing control, unable to reverse the certain collapse. Somehow I knew I was going to fall short. Perhaps it was this last recognition of defeat that finally tipped off the short-circuit within my mind. After a lifetime of fighting for success, striving for recognition and position, here I was in front of over a hundred of my peers, all waiting for me to perform. My legs felt weak, my hands trembled, and my voice was halting as the slides began. I tried to cover up by simply using the slides as cue cards—a last desperate effort to save myself from humiliation. And then it happened.

I remember vividly those terrifying moments. Looking at the slides for guidance, I could no longer connect one thought with the next. I could read the words, but they made no sense. The path of intelligent communication had gone haywire. I didn't know it at the time, but I was experiencing an epileptic seizure.

In retrospect I can imagine the disconnection between the layered anatomical subdivisions of my brain. It was as if the various sections of an orchestra were isolated in sound and sight from each other, the resulting music no longer in time or tune with the other parts. My thought processes were misguided, disharmonious, without apparent connections—lost parts searching unsuccessfully for one another like children separated from their parents amidst a large crowd. I knew that my mind was badly out of sync.

I was still able to speak in simple sentences. I could walk and had an awareness of my surroundings, but for someone used to functioning on a highly intellectual level, I felt as if I had momentarily returned to preschool. I excused myself from the speaker's podium, still vainly attempting to hide my illness, announcing that I simply did not feel well. Colleagues sat me in a chair in the corridor outside the hall, where well-meaning physicians offered me water, orange juice, and a barrage of questions and possible diagnoses. I was too embarrassed to tell them that I was dreadfully ill. No one there—including myself—had any idea what was going on, but I am told that I soon answered everyone's questions by having a full-blown, flailing, unconscious epileptic fit—a *grand mal* seizure.

It seems one can retain memory of events occurring during partial complex epilepsy, which was what had first happened while I was on the podium. But a grand mal event is forgiving in that it disconnects whatever disc it is that stores memory in the brain.

Recalling all of this now, I am moved in many ways.

I am humiliated and shamed because I've seen grand mal seizures with patients of my own and it means that there was an ugly, flailing, slobbering, animal-like distortion of my body. Yet at the same time I am emotionally separated from this event because my knowledge of it is imagined and not actually imbedded in memory. My imagination allows me to see myself as the sick patient, vainly striving to regain control over his own mind and body. Only the pain of a dislocated shoulder remained to give me physical evidence of the fury of the uncontrolled dishevelment of neuronal activity that others had the unpleasant happenstance of witnessing.

I vaguely remember going through all the necessary tests: the poking and probing, the foley catheter in my bladder, the lumbar puncture in my spine, the intravenous line that infiltrated my arm. I have flash memories of the helicopter ride to the hospital, the reassuring voice of a friend in the plane, and later the eerie, futuristic feeling as I was rolled into the CT scanner. Though I realized they were looking for a brain tumor, I was too sick to care and too drugged to be afraid.

The fear came later. Only after my mind was again synchronized could it begin to project the potential effects of this terrible illness on my career, my family, my income, and my self-esteem.

During the days afterward in the hospital, I was emotionally fragile and tears came at the mere sight of a close friend or loved one. It is natural for emotions to be uncontrolled and changeable with certain diseases of the central nervous system. I was embarrassed and ashamed, but unable to control my emotional responses because my unsettled and drugged mind would not let me. I remember an overwhelming sadness, a desperate need to apologize as if I had simply let everyone down.

On my first weekend home after I was discharged, my daughters showed me the kites they had made with one of our neighbors. He had risen to the occasion and substituted for their dad. The girls had flown the kites in a contest across the valley and they told me how frightened they had been when they had looked up toward the hospital knowing I was in one of those rooms. They had gone through the motions of enjoyment, holding on to their youthful spirit, thanks to the strength and courage of their mom and our family friends.

As is the case with so many of my patients, the spouse paid the greatest price for my illness—perhaps pays it still. My wife, Molly, experienced fear for me—yes—but also for our family, our income, our children's future. She exhibited courage on the outside, but I know she felt pain and uncertainty on the inside.

I began a rapid recovery, covering up my feelings as well, not willing to show weakness to my wife. I was determined to return immediately to work to prove to others—and to myself—that I had not been beaten by the attack. In my hurried effort to put this painful episode behind me, I failed to think of her anguish and fear.

Looking back, Molly now remembers resentment at having been seemingly ignored during all the concern for me. No one ever asked how she was holding up. No one kept her adequately informed about my test results or prognosis. Most of all, she remembers her uncertainty about bringing me home at a time when I was still tranquilized on drugs, with no one spending adequate time reassuring her and instructing her as to my condition and what to expect.

It is years now since the seizure. One minor recurrence early on allowed my neurologists to pinpoint their diagnosis and more specifically prescribe medication that has held in check this aberration of the mind that so threatens me.

During that last event I was fully conscious throughout, aware now what the bizarre confusion represented and therefore able to walk myself right over to the doctor's office and suggest he hook me up to the electroencephalography (EEG) equipment and have a look. This time they put me in an intensive-care bed with EEG wires glued to my head. Then I learned what true humiliation is, as team after team of doctors—many personally known to me—crowded into the room to watch my mind dance. Massive doses of intravenous valium succeeded only in making me deathly nauseated. I wretched convulsively as my brain continued its dysrhythmia. I remember being unable to urinate while lying down and the humbling experience of having to ask my wife to hold me up while I emptied my bladder into a urinal as I clumsily missed the mark. I can only imagine the renewed fears, uncertainties, and ambivalence in her mind as she stood there in that room, knowing then for certain that the possibility of recurrence of my epileptic fits would be always with us.

Again I rebounded immediately. The inner force of pride, my drive for success, the spirit of a man undaunted refused to allow me to be taken down. Yes, I am proud of my resilience and fortitude, but I also know now what I did not understand then: that in my drive for self-preservation I unwittingly ignored the needs of those closest to me, especially my wife. In consciously refusing to recognize and admit my fear, I isolated myself emotionally from family and friends, driving a wedge not yet fully removed.

I see this pattern repeatedly in my own patients: the dynamics of relationships altered by serious illness. I have no obvious advice to give, for I myself am still trying to undo the damage in my own life.

In the months that followed my seizures, I learned how fear becomes the most debilitating symptom of disease. My confidence waned and with it the assurance in my voice, the quickness of my mind, the decisiveness of my actions, the strength of my convictions. The anxiety that accompanied fear brought a timidity of gait, a slight dampness of skin, a fine tremor of hand—all exacerbated by stress. I became unsure of myself because I was uncertain of the future and—like most patients—I began to concern myself unproductively with a future I had no power to control.

In those activities at which I excel—such as bedside doctor-patient communication and performing cardiac catheterization laboratory procedures—I regained my confidence most easily and quickly, for in my pre-epilepsy life these were the things in which I was most secure. But in other public functions—such as teaching, giving lectures, singing in church, socializing at parties—I was much more hesitant, afraid that somehow my disability would show. I was self-conscious, insecure, and afraid to fail in public. Fear haunted me as a ghost, ever-present, consuming, unnerving; and yet even then I did not understand fear as I do now.

Without fanfare or forethought Molly, still struggling with her own doubts, opened the door for me as we prepared to go to bed one evening: "You just have to give it all to God, John. He'll take this weight off your shoulders." I lay there all that night letting those words sink in as she went off to sleep, not knowing how profound a truth she had articulated. That night I discovered the simple, healing beauty of "letting go," a truth that has become an integral part of my life and my practice of medicine. The very next morning, I left for work with a magical serenity and calmness, a newfound inner peace that restored my confidence and sense of self. I felt physically restored, unburdened, on course again after a wayward storm.

There were no trumpets, no balloons, no flashing lights. There was no change, yet I had changed. There was no struggle, for my struggle was ended. There was no gift, for it had already been given.

If by my writing I can impart but one idea, open one door, it would be to convince those facing serious illness to let go. It is not just my patients but their families, their friends, their ministers, their doctors and nurses I want to convince that letting go is the gift of healing that comes only from God. We physicians cannot expect technology and science to accomplish the goal of healing alone; our ministering must be accompanied by the simple truth—given not earned, accepted not purchased—that God is love and that all we need do to receive God's love is to let go.

I have learned that letting go does not mean giving up or caving in. Those treatments available for a particular illness should be undertaken. The mysteries of life being revealed ever so slowly to scientists must always be pursued.

Those things we can change, alter, medicate, or remove, we should. However, to spend one's life (or one's practice) asking "what if this happens" or "what if that happens" is paramount to a life sentence of unhappiness, frustration, fear, and anxiety. Those things we cannot control must be accepted. We must work only on those things we can change, not on those we cannot.

In letting go, there is a second step that allows us to verify the true healing of the first. Having let go of ourselves and our future, we must direct all of our energy and time toward helping others. This step is as important as the first. In suffering ourselves, we learn how to better serve those who suffer also. I now see my illness as a gift that has brought with it a wisdom only earned by personal experience. Thanks to my illness, I can now pass on to my patients this truth: in loving, we are loved; in pardoning, we are pardoned; in giving, we receive; and in exalting, we are exalted.

TWO

STEPHEN'S FAMILY

Stephen is the kind of man that makes a doctor's life easy, because he never complains, he simply accepts. I treat this fifty-year-old for chronic but controlled angina.

Pain and suffering is nothing new to Stephen. Maybe that's why he considers his illness just another small burden, certainly not anything he'll allow to interrupt his responsibilities to his family.

There's a longing for freedom in Stephen's eyes, a look of acceptance tempered by a faint mist of unhappiness to which he will not give in. His daughter, Jennifer, now thirty years old, has been an invalid since childhood due to polio. She is confined to bed or chair, with no control of her bowel or bladder. The young woman is able to converse but is otherwise totally dependent. She requires a special van for transportation and usually just stays at home.

Stephen's wife, Lorraine, is completely engrossed with caring for their daughter. Stephen tells me it's easier for him than for his wife, because he at least gets to go to work and to hunt or bowl with friends once and a while. Lorraine is always at home and has no other life.

Serious illness has affected the couple's relationship. They experience frustration, periods of love-hate ambivalence when emotions surface and tempers flare. But their love always wins out.

Years ago, the family tried to become active in a church, thinking that might bring some help and support for their daughter, but they soon gave up that expectation. Others in the congregation were kind but clearly shied away from contact with a situation that made them so uncomfortable. It was easier to avoid Stephen's family than to deal with them, not just because it was difficult to know what to do for them but because the parishioners were afraid of facing their own vulnerability and mortality.

And so life goes on for Stephen and his family, alone in their little world of suffering that no one else can begin to understand. The pain is so deep, so old, so lasting that Stephen does not even bring it up anymore. I have to ask how he is coping.

A nurse comes once a week for an afternoon to be with Jennifer so that Stephen and Lorraine can rush away from their prison, free to shop, to drive around aimlessly, to be anywhere but home. Stephen tells me these brief respites are like holidays or vacations.

Stephen accepts and lives with his own disease very well. He doesn't have time for fear or self-pity. His energy is focused on helping the others who need him. His inner strength derives from his selflessness. Every day I am struck by the fortitude of my patients and wonder where their spiritual strength comes from.

I have so much to learn from Stephen and his family, and what I have to give is so little in comparison.

THREE

DAVID

David is one of the nicest patients in my practice. Many years ago, he suffered a large heart attack from which he recovered nicely. Later he developed a mild angina syndrome that caused moderate limitation on his activity. The pain was quite predictable, however, and did not keep him from working. I did an elective cardiac catheterization on David in order to assess his long term management plan and decided that conservative (that is, no surgery) treatment was best.

David has done remarkably well. He is now sixty-five, retired, and only gets his angina pains when walking outside in bitter cold weather or when he pushes his exercise well past his normal everyday level. He has been very happy leading an active, very near normal life. He has come to accept his disease and to live with it rather than struggle against it. Over the years, the two of us have developed a rather close relationship.

A few years back, David's son-in-law died of cancer. David's daughter, Alex, and his two young granddaughters now live with David and his wife, Marie, who have been together now for forty-six years. The grandkids have essentially become like their own children, so there has been no time for David and Marie to get old.

If anything can keep David active and young-at-heart, his grandchildren will. He cuddles them, disciplines them, spoils them—and feels as responsible for them as if he were only thirty and parenting for the first time. These are lucky little girls to have such a "dad"—softened, wizened, experienced by his years.

Yet David is also one lucky grandpa. How many of us get a chance to do it all again—the dolls, the Christmas stockings, the first bicycles, the Easter bonnets, the birthday parties, the first days of school?

Today David arrived at my office unannounced, wanting to be seen. I was on hospital calls with no clinic time scheduled and I did not immediately connect the name given me over the phone with David's story. My memory for names has always been very bad. I need a face and a chart to somehow turn on the circuit in my mind that holds my memories of patients. It doesn't take much; often I just need to see the face or read my last brief scribbled note. All the little details then miraculously spring back into focus as if a switch had been turned on.

Another of my faults is my need for order and predictability in my day. Although I am constantly behind in my schedule because I tend to spend so much time with each patient, I am able to work through a crowded waiting room as well as the next doctor; but on such days I know ahead of time how many patients are to be seen and pace my work accordingly. I do not, however, deal well with surprises, unexpected changes, or interruptions.

And so my first reaction when the nurses called to inform me that a patient expected to be seen with no appointment was one of irritation. I always feel guilty afterwards for having had initial reactions of anger when disturbed from one project in order to see an unscheduled patient, because as soon as I have recovered my memory of that person and heard the reason he or she has come I am inevitably glad the person did.

In this case, I find that five days ago, David had several episodes of vertigo (a condition of dizziness in which the individual or his or her surroundings seem to whirl around in a circular fashion). It is rarely serious and usually caused by a temporary inflammation or imbalance of the inner ear.

Dizziness related to the heart, on the other hand, is more of a black-out or near black-out situation. David had had no palpitations and no chest pain. Looking back in his chart, I see that he has had problems with vertigo in the past. In fact, ten years ago he saw me for an identical episode. Since then he has had occasional "dizzy" feelings that come and go with no rhyme or reason.

David's blood pressure is fine; his heart rhythm regular, his examination unchanged from just a month ago when I saw him for a routine visit. After a good review of his symptoms, I ask David whether there is any new stress in his life, any change at home that has him upset. He thinks about it for a few moments and then answers no. Yes, he says, his younger brother died several months back of a heart attack and this has been "pretty hard to take," but we had talked about this at some length on his last visit and he seemed to be dealing with his grief in a normal manner.

David maintains that there is no new stress, no new emotional upset, no recent event that should be a factor. He believes all this to be true, but I am sure there has to be some subtle change in his life and simply continue to listen. As we talk more, the situation becomes quite obvious.

Ever since the mild recurrence of his vertigo five days ago, there has indeed been a change in David's home life. It has been the reemergence of fear. Marie and Alex have begun begging David to go see his doctor. He tells me on further questioning that his daughter said to him, "Daddy, I just don't know what we'd ever do without you."

Fear, once present in chronic disease, can never be taken away completely. It may be shoved aside and even forgotten as one gets back to daily living, personal goals, projects, and loved ones. But fear is always present just underneath the surface, ready to return at the slightest calling, capable of snowballing again into the ugly, unforgiving, relentless destroyer of life it can be. Fear can be present yet unseen, unrecognized yet all-consuming, hidden yet totally incapacitating.

David's family, inadvertently and with the best of intentions, has started all over again the totally counterproductive practice of trying to restrict a patient's activity in the name of showing their concern: "Why don't you lie down for a while?" "You better not tackle that job today." "Let us do it, you just rest." "Are you sure you feel all right?" "We don't want anything happening to you."

Though David would almost certainly be able to deal with his own brief resurfacing of fear about his illness, the uprising of fear and protectiveness all around him finally has led to what it always leads to. David's self-confidence has begun to erode and he begins to ask himself questions: "Should I be driving?" "I wonder if there really is something wrong again?" "What would happen to those little girls if I die?"

Because of my own illness, I have known such fear and live with it still. I have seen my own fear resurface, cause anxiety and its accompanying symptoms, then submerge again as life goes on—in hiding yet always ready to pounce. When fear returns, I experience a vague lightheadedness, a faint nausea or queasiness, a jittery feeling that cannot be pinpointed. I know something is wrong but am never sure what that something is.

David and I talk for much longer than I'd planned, and the more we talk the clearer it is to me that his medical status has not changed at all. All David needs is reassurance to restore his confidence and push his fear back where it belongs.

At the end of our conversation, David says, "You must know, Doctor, that it is good to have someone to talk to and I thank you a lot for that. When you're a dad and your own dad has died, there just isn't anyone to talk to about your own problems because you're responsible for everyone else's."

I have known these feelings as well.

FOUR

JANET

Three years ago, Janet developed pain in her lower chest that sounded like gallbladder trouble. At the same time, though, abnormalities on her EKG (electrocardiogram test) suggested that her heart might be the source of the pain. As it turned out, Janet had both problems.

We'll never know for certain how much of her pain was from her gallstones and how much was from her heart, but what matters is that other doctors and I were able to get her back on her feet again. I performed an angioplasty on the blocked artery in her heart; then just a few weeks later the general surgeons were able to safely remove her gallbladder. Janet has had no more pain from her medical problems and is living the active life of a busy, sixty-three-year-old grandmother without fear.

Janet has pain of a different kind, however. Her husband, George, is an alcoholic. Over the years, alcohol has driven a wedge between them, causing them to drift apart. Recently, however, one of their daughters was physically abused by the couple's son-in-law. This ugly incident has led to the daughter's divorce, but ironically it has brought Janet and George back closer again as they have faced this family crisis together. Their daughter has moved back in with them, and their beautiful blond-haired, blue-eyed granddaughter now lives with them as well. She is Janet's pride and joy.

Today while examining Janet, I hear a new left carotid bruit (a sound suggesting some artery disease in the carotid artery in her neck). The severity is unknown. She's had no symptoms of neurological deficit at all, and even if I knew that there was a significant blockage the treatment would be only to take a mild blood thinner (such as aspirin), which Janet is already on. Only if symptoms such as dizziness or transient loss of vision occurred would surgery be necessary. That is the current medical thinking on the subject.

So, do I tell Janet about her new condition? Do I order tests to try to confirm the carotid disease? And if I do test, what would I do with the results? The one thing I know would happen is that I would create fear of a stroke in Janet, and that would be a disease unto itself. Right now she is happy, fulfilled, active. If there were a definitive treatment that could prevent stroke and prolong life in this case, then there's no question I would investigate and consider it. And if Janet were having neurological symptoms that were interfering with her enjoyment of life despite the blood thinner, then I would definitely recommend more action. Right now, though, Janet indicates no basis for further medical intervention.

Again, the only result of my testing and investigating the new finding at this point would be the creation of fear. I would be causing suffering rather than alleviating it. And so I make the decision not to tell Janet what I heard, and I will live with that decision. I will live with the fear for her.

In the waiting room after our appointment, Janet calls me over to meet her daughter. The signs of her fractured cheek bone, incurred during the brutal beating, are still very much in evidence. Standing next to Janet's daughter is her beautiful three-and-a-half-year-old granddaughter, hugging a doll close to her chest. The little girl is shy at first, but brightens up when I bend down to chat. I ask if Santa had brought her the doll. "No, my grandma did," the child answers.

Janet beams with pride, and somehow I know that, for this moment at least, my instincts have been right.

FIVE

MEGAN AND GRANDPA

Megan has light brown hair pulled back tightly beneath a yellow band and then left to fall gently with an inward curl that frames a thin face. Colored glasses do not hide her eagerness, nor her fear. She is in her mid-twenties and dressed demurely in a suit that is worn with the slight awkwardness that those who dress up infrequently often exhibit. Somehow I find Meagan very appealing—this young woman here with her grandfather for a visit with his heart specialist.

Megan sits next to him—taut, straining to display a mature, professional composure, determined to be in control—while inside she weeps and trembles with uncertainty. Grandpa, meanwhile, is quite relaxed, dressed in a loose brown-patterned sportshirt, his undershirt showing at the neck. He also wears glasses—wire rims—and his thinning hair is all white. He shows every bit of his seventy-nine years, perhaps even a bit more. His eyes are tired, his cheeks sallow, his posture slumped.

Yet there is an immediately visible sense of calmness about this man—an aura of acceptance, of wisdom, of inner peace. His skin is parchment-thin and has the transparency and colorless, turgorless, wrinkled appearance that only time bestows—age spots and engorged veins seeming to stand out in relief.

I had been forewarned of the situation by their family doctor, a former resident of mine who is a good, caring physician but young and perhaps not yet able to speak of death. There are many occasions when it is the physician's duty to recognize that it is time to allow life to take its natural course to death . . . and to help those involved to let go. Megan is a coronary care nurse, knowledgeable and proud, trained to sustain life in the face of heart disease. She works in a smaller community hospital where the medical teams stabilize patients and then whenever possible transfer them to a major medical center such as ours, where modern miracles of technology and surgery can be performed in order that suffering may be relieved and death forestalled.

Megan's understanding of these modern interventions comes from journals that boast of medical interventions that can be done. There is never any realistic discussion in these publications of the failures and the numerous occasions in which, in our insistence upon doing something—anything—when death seems inevitable, we only create more suffering by prolonging death. Why is it so much more comfortable for all of us to think and act as if we can control our destiny than to recognize the truth, speak of our limitations, share our feelings of love, and concentrate more on what *is* rather than what *might be*?

Grandpa had a large heart attack several weeks ago. His heart muscle was irrevocably damaged by the event, and for whatever time he has left he will be physically much more limited than before. But no one can predict what time course Grandpa's life will take, what winds, tides, currents may yet shift before his family will have to say a final, painful, sorrowful goodbye. As a physician, I can try to prevent or limit Grandpa's pain and help him adapt to a new pace of life, but to pretend that I can do something for him now that will forestall death would be unfair to myself and to him.

Megan is reacting out of love. She is the medically trained member of a family who all fear that their patriarch's death is near. She feels responsible to Grandpa and to her whole clan to make sure that everything possible is being done for him. Most of all she feels responsible to herself for she is convinced that modern science is better than it is. She wills it to be so; she needs it to be so. She depends on her unrealistic expectations because the alternative is too painful for her to bear: this wonderful man whom she loves so dearly must one day leave us, despite all our hopes and efforts to the contrary.

Megan speaks what is on her mind: "But there might be another blockage. And if he has another attack, he . . . what if there's more? If we find it now we can fix it before anything else happens." Megan tries to maintain her composure, but tears well up in her eyes as we quietly discuss the options, the risks, the limitations.

Grandpa is not having any pain now. He can walk around and involve himself in family activities. If he were suffering pain, then any procedure, at any risk, would be worthy of consideration for the purpose of relieving that pain. But such procedures are not indicated.

Grandpa knows all of this before it is said. "I came here today because Megan told me I should. I want her to be happy. I've had a good life; I'm not afraid of dying. If I had a lot of pain, then I suppose I'd want you to do something." These are his feelings—simply put, calmly pronounced. Grandpa doesn't want any more medical procedures.

By now the conversation has shifted back to Megan. Because of her background, I feel the need to go into great detail concerning my opinion. Grandpa stands up and very politely asks to be excused: "Perhaps it would be best if I left you two alone for a while. I don't understand any of this anyhow."

So he sits in the hall outside my office while I discuss the medical aspects of the situation with Megan. She tearfully confesses that this was pretty much what she expected to hear, but that she was hoping for more: "It's hard enough taking care of dying patients, but when it's someone you love . . . ."

We finish talking and start to walk down the hall. When we get to her grandfather, he grabs her by both arms and looks deep into her eyes. "I love you so much, Megan," he says. "I love you too, Grandpa," she cries. I leave these two beautiful people—separated by years but joined forever by their love—hugging each other.

It is not until I get back into my own office alone that I allow my own tears to fall. They feel good.

SIX

WARREN'S STORE

Warren has had a heart attack and lives with some mild angina, but on a relatively simple program of medication, this seventy-six-year-old is stable and ambulatory. The only thing I need to do is write new prescriptions for him and send him home with a lot of reassurance that he's doing just fine.

Let me tell you about Warren's home. About ten or twelve years ago, he and his wife, Linda, put their money into a little antique shop they opened up in their small town. Warren had worked hard as an accountant for many years, so the purpose of the antique shop was not to make money; it was to give Warren and Linda something fun and exciting to do in their retirement years. They had talked about it, planned and saved, gone on buying trips, decorated the shop, and opened a small but classy business—together. They moved into the apartment above their own store. They had pride, satisfaction, joy, and purpose. They were happy.

Then Linda succumbed to cancer. Heartbreak, loneliness, darkness, a period of grief overtook Warren. But there was still his store—their store—for him. There was buying to be done, a business to be run, goals to be met. Warren got himself going, as all survivors must, and life went on.

Just as Warren was beginning to bounce back, however, he was pushed down again. Two months after Linda died, he was hit with his heart attack. He seemed depressed and anxious in the hospital, and someone asked a psychiatrist to see him. The doctors labeled him as having "an adjustment disorder," for which they gave him drugs. Side effects from these drugs affected Warren's memory, and the doctors simply added "confusion" to his list of diagnoses.

Warren finally got home and was starting the long road back to recovery when he was slapped down again. This time he had a stroke. He was hospitalized again and seemed depressed, so this time he was labeled as having "agitated depression."

I look at Warren's chart and shake my head. This man lost his wife, made it through a heart attack and then a stroke. Who wouldn't be depressed?

Most of the medical notes I'm reading have no social history at all. Some mention that Warren drinks some alcohol. Another says he "works" at an antique shop. "Works at a antique shop!" That store is his life. It's all he has left. The most discouraging entry in his chart is the one that lists "personality disorder" as a formal diagnosis.

It was nearly five years ago that Warren lost his Linda, then faced death himself. I wonder at his strength. I feel for the man. I want so much to help him.

The doctors had saved his life, but for what? For the store, obviously. There is still the store. Warren's life can be good again. All of us need a purpose, something to live for, something to get better for. For Warren there is but one such goal: the store, his store, their store.

Warren will get back to work. It will be slow going. His

family is convinced now that he is incapable of running the store. They will push him and badger him, trying to get him to give up the business. But how can he? He understands that this is his last hope, all that is left for him. He can do it. He knows he can. I know he can.

Not for money.

For life.

CODA

The years went on and Warren kept his antique store going. But he was constantly ridiculed, told he was too "senile" to run a business; told he must sell. Then came a buyer, a lawyer, a bank . . . and the whole thing was done. All Warren had to do was sign an agreement, but he would not. He resisted and the more he fought the more he was told he was senile, crazy, incapable. The deal was reworked by the buyer to include Warren's being able to stay in the apartment upstairs, where he and Linda had been so happy. Finally, under pressure, the "senile old man" signed away his life, his dream, his reason for being: his and Linda's store. There he lives now, up in the apartment above someone else's store, silent, with no one to see, nothing to do.

Much time has passed. Warren's medical condition remains really quite good. But the man is alone with his memories and dwells in the past, for the past is all that he has. Bitterness, hatred, unhappiness all simmer inside him daily as he spends his endless days alone. He has no new challenge, no tomorrow to work for or plan for. He feels rejected. He knows that he is perceived as a "failure," "useless," "waiting to die." Warren has lost his pride and his desire. He lives now within a self-imposed web of loneliness, blaming others for his unhappiness; for were he to blame himself, he could not live another day.

Warren doesn't fish or hunt or paint or garden. His life was his business. He still needs to have a role, a service, a function in his life, where he can still use his knowledge and feel productive. If the medical profession could find for Warren a function that would give him back his pride, then we would have really helped him.

We could give this man back his life . . . if we cared enough to take the time to love him.

SEVEN

DONALD AND CHAPPY

Donald has become a friend over all these years. He has had a chance to watch me grow and change in my job as I have watched him. Donald, now eighty years old, gets very demanding, gruff, and sometimes rude when things don't go his way; he's learned that at a big hospital it's the only way to be heard. But deep down, Donald is a blubbering, sensitive softie who enjoys being more than just a patient with me.

Ten years ago, Donald had bypass surgery. He still has some angina, but it's manageable and life goes on. His wife, Grace, has been through cancer treatments and seems to be doing well. They've both known the of fear of facing death.

Shortly after I met Donald, he lost a close friend—his old dog. He was devastated, down, swore he'd never get another one. I was perhaps a little helpful in convincing him to get a new dog, which he named after me: "Chappy." Chappy and Donald are inseparable. They take long walks every day and do almost everything together. Donald is proud of his dog, and brags about how smart he is.

Today, though, Donald gets teary-eyed when he speaks of Chappy. For now the dog is losing his sight from cataracts and will need surgery. Again Donald tells me he'll never get another dog. "What would happen to a new dog if I died?" he asks. "There would be no one to care for him."

Donald loves his canine friend so much. Chappy's upcoming surgery is a major emotional stress. "Never again," Donald cries, with tears coming close but not breaking.

I am convinced that Chappy is the reason Donald has done so well—both physically and emotionally. It is loving and caring for others that keeps us young. It is having others who depend on us that gives us strength and lifts us up when we're down. Will Donald get another dog if Chappy were to die? Of course he will, even if I have to get one for him myself!

As our session draws toward a close, Donald looks me in the eye and says, "You know, there's something different about you now than there was back eleven years ago when we met. You seem to be a Christian now."

I think Donald is right. My own life experience, illness, frailties, victories, and defeats have changed the person I am perceived to be by my patients.

I have aged and grown spiritually with them. I suppose I do now verbalize my faith in God in a way I never did when I did not understand the real meaning of being a doctor. I do now profess a faith in God that grows daily, though my doubts persist.

EIGHT

CHAPPY'S DEATH

I'm glad Donald is the last patient on my schedule today, not only because I need a lot of time with him, but also because it is a very emotional visit that results in a lot of tears . . . my own included.

Donald's dog, Chappy, died just a few weeks ago. He'd had cataract surgery and there were complications, then seizures at home, then back to the vet's where Donald and his wife, Grace, left the dog overnight for tests.

The next day they waited and waited for a call, then finally went to the clinic, thinking they would be able to bring their friend home. But on their arrival, they were drawn aside and with no warning told that Chappy had passed away.

With tears in their eyes and feeling lost, Donald and Grace asked for their dog's remains, gently placing the body on the back seat of the car. They drove around aimlessly for a little while, finally deciding to bury Chappy in their own yard. Donald went to a good friend's store and asked if one of the man's sons might be able to come over to the house to dig a hole. His friend asked him why and Donald broke down, explaining that he needed to bury his dog. The man was obviously a true friend and understood; he closed his store immediately and went home with Donald to dig the grave himself. Donald and Grace found a good wooden box, covered it with plastic on top and underneath, then picked a single rose from the garden and laid it on the box, saying goodbye to their faithful friend before the grave was closed.

"I left the back yard that day and haven't been back since," Donald tells me. Grace, up until now sitting quietly in the corner, speaks up: "I have. I go out and talk to Chappy every day. I feel like I just have to."

By now all three of us are crying and reaching for tissue, as if somehow wiping away the tears would take the sorrow away. I pull out a short piece I'd written six months ago. It had been written at a time when my own dog, Tasha, was at the same vet's, dying. I feel Donald might like to read what I had written. I don't know why. Maybe I want to share with him my own feelings about my Tasha, that somehow reading this will make Donald feel less alone in his grief.

Our session goes on and on, finally getting around to an examination and discussion of Donald's medical status, which seems fine. We keep coming back to Chappy, though, with feelings expressed that are much more vital to Donald's health than any "check-up" I can render.

Donald feels guilty for letting the dog go for surgery. He remembers reading somewhere that even blind dogs should not be put to sleep, that all they live for is the scent of their master. There is also an airing of hurt feelings between husband and wife. Somehow Donald and Grace feel comfortable dealing with these in my presence, whereas they probably have not been able to do so at home. Sometimes a doctor serves that role, as mediator or referee between loved ones.

Just days after their loss, Donald had realized he would have to have another dog. He found one, but this time it was Grace who was not ready. She was still going out in the back yard to talk with Chappy and was not ready to embrace a new friend yet. The old was still too close.

Donald was hurt that Grace held him back. As couples do, they are bickering about their feelings, each loving the other, each needing the other, but both also needing to vent their frustrations.

There will soon be another dog for Donald and Grace; there must be. But there also must be a time to weep, a time to remember, a time for the pain to ease. Donald needs to go into his back yard and face his pain, allow his tears to fall, and realize he can never replace his old friend . . . only make a new one. They need some time before they get a new dog, and Grace knowingly tells Donald that when they are ready they should name their dog Lucky—"Lucky to have you."

NINE

LAWRENCE

Lawrence has come to my office today for a check-up on his eighty-one-year-old heart. A year ago his wife, Betty, suffered a stroke, and she has been an invalid in a nearby nursing home—not able to speak or respond, caught somewhere between life and death, a living ghost.

Lawrence has visited his wife every single day, squeezing her hand to try to insure her knowledge of his presence. His love and devotion have never wavered, but his hopes for tomorrow fade into memories of yesterday. Betty appears to be lost, suspended in seemingly endless non-life.

Helpless and in awe of his strength, Lawrence's children, friends, and physicians all wait with him for the final curtain that must surely fall. Time has allowed Lawrence's mind to grasp the reality of Betty's situation, yet his heart holds out, giving untiringly until her death comes.

The doctors in charge of Betty's care have moved her out of the nursing home and back into our acute care hospital. They have given her intravenous fluids and are feeding her through a tube in her stomach. I was not aware of her admission until today, but in the middle of my usual check-up with Lawrence a nurse calls me out rather frantically on a matter that cannot wait.

Lawrence's daughter, Shirley, trembling and uncertain, needs to talk to me alone. The doctors have "called for a formal meeting" so that a decision can be made about stopping Betty's intravenous and feeding tubes. "I just don't know what to do. Wouldn't that be like starving her?" she asks. Tearfully Shirley tells me of her own dilemma, then concentrates on her dad, Lawrence: "What would this decision do to him? I don't know if he can stand it."

I don't understand why we must always have "meetings" and "group decisions" about such an obvious choice. We must allow death to be part of life. Death does not mean failure; it is natural. Death is not an end; it is the beginning of more life. Death is not ugly; it can and should be beautiful, if allowed to occur in quiet dignity. The physician must simply allow death to come and help create a setting in which the mystery, the tears, the memories, the pain, and the love can be shared by those who care . . . whose lives have been touched by the deceased.

When I return to the office after talking all of this out with Shirley, Lawrence and I first finish up a review and examination concentrating on him. Then I gradually shift the conversation over to his wife's situation. It is obvious that Lawrence is ready. He was not expecting to discuss the issue with me, for I am not caring for his wife; but perhaps he is more comfortable doing so with me because of the mutual feeling of trust that we have developed.

I suppose it is natural for relationships between doctors and patients to grow rich over the years—to become more open, more honest, more rewarding over time. A physician may only see a particular patient twice a year, but with each visit the doctor becomes more and more a part of that individual's life. There is a trusting zone that allows freedom of expression—a development in the relationship beyond which truth emerges, love supplants empathy, extrication from emotional involvement is no longer possible.

Lawrence knew the question of letting his wife go would come; he also knows the answer: "She would not want to live like this." He had been struggling for a year now, not wanting to face the truth, but he acknowledges it now: "All we're doing is making life worse for her now. I know she's not going to make it."

When it is time to withhold further medical care from a loved one, the physician merely has to allow a family to express their thoughts.

The answer is usually already there, being held secretly inside as if to voice it would be to break one's solemn pledge of love. Once these feelings are released from bondage, however, there is a sense of relief that accompanies the pain and sorrow of death.

The hug I give to and receive from Lawrence at that moment make the rest of what I have to do today seem inconsequential. Lawrence and I walk slowly down the hall to return to his wife's side, afraid yet somehow prepared now for what must be and able to take his daughter's hand in mutual support.

TEN

DANIEL

I watch Daniel walk down the hall toward my office and know even before examining him that I will have little to offer—other than my time and caring.

Daniel is thirty-one-years-old and weighs three hundred and sixty-five pounds. His portentous size evokes stares of awe and feelings of pity, for his gait is ungainly and noticeable. His great mass glides from side to side as he walks, creating a constant counter-motion to the forward direction he is striving for. His appearance is out of sync—fluid yet awkward, human yet elephantine.

Daniel's doctor referred him to me in order to check on his heart. Some minor changes on his electrocardiogram and possible enlargement of his heart on a chest x-ray had raised the possibility of heart disease, but Daniel has no specific symptoms. His doctor just wants a specialist to review the findings. Obesity can cause abnormalities of the heart, but the further I delve into Daniel's medical history, the more convinced I become that the primary problem here is Daniel's weight . . . or is it?

Daniel had gone to college for a year and a half, planning to major in religion. During his sophomore year, however, he was called home to a tragedy: his five-year-old baby brother had drowned accidentally in a swimming pool. Somehow, Daniel blames himself for this unspeakable loss. "If I hadn't left home, it wouldn't have happened," he insists. And now, years later, he is caught up in a quagmire of self-inflicted pain, depression, and stagnation. He hates himself for not having done anything significant with his life and feels embarrassed because he is still dependent on his parents. Yet Daniel is still afraid to break out. "If I leave, something terrible will happen again," he tells me. Most of all, Daniel is lonely. He works as a clerk, then returns home to his parents. He has no wife, no girlfriend, no real friends.

"Me, a girlfriend? A wife? Look at me!" he shouts. "Do you think anyone would want to be with me?" Daniel's eyes glisten with tears he keeps just below the surface. The wound is deep, but Daniel cannot mask the pain. He lives with a ghost, but the ghost is not his dead brother; it is the ghost of fear.

There are special programs at some locations around the country where obesity problems are addressed by long-term therapy that would require Daniel's moving there for several months. He has considered these, and we talked at length about committing to such a course. He is only thirty-one; something must be done. But it must start with Daniel himself. The goal here is not to prevent heart disease; that would be a secondary benefit. The primary objective is to help Daniel find confidence in himself—a parcel of happiness, a glimpse of light in his darkness.

It seems to me that his going to a special program away from home is the only sensible step for him to take at this crucial crossroad. He could find another job at his new location, start a new life while working on his eating problem, make exercise a part of his life, and—most important of all—face his fear. Daniel's parents are getting older; they will not live forever.

He must not be allowed to blame himself for any future illness in their home. I suspect it will require constant emotional support and therapy from a professional to help Daniel deal with the reality of that situation now, not later when a tragic event at home could send him hurtling downward again.

Confidence, fulfillment, pride, happiness, love, friendship—how lightly we take these gifts for granted. Here is a man who has none of these.

I ask Daniel if he has asked God for help and he replies, "Which one?" Daniel is uncertain about religion: "I think I like the Buddhists the most because they preach against killing. And yet in school I liked the Catholics. Ever since my brother died I just haven't been very interested in God."

Toward the end of our session, Daniel reaches into his pocket and pulls out a medal—St. Christopher, I believe—fondles it for several minutes in silence, then stands up to leave. "I do carry this wherever I go," he says. "I just feel better with it. I know there must be a God—somewhere."

After Daniel leaves. I feel rather tired and empty as I try to write out his history and relate my recommendations to his own doctor. How much do I say? I did no tests, prescribed no pills, gave no lecture. All I really did was listen to a young man I had come to care for, to grieve for, to hurt for.

CODA

It is Christmas now, two months after I saw Daniel. New snow fell last night, enough to decorate the barren branches with a promise of beauty and love for tomorrow. A card comes to my office: two angels—one holding a branch with buds springing to life with flower, the other a holy book. "Joyous Christmas," it says, and in Daniel's own hand, "I just wanted to thank you for seeing me, and being so nice to me. Who knows, maybe this time I'll make it."

Nice to him, that's all I was. May God bring him the gifts I cannot bring.

ELEVEN

ANNA AND PETER

It is Christmas time. Anna and Peter wait patiently for me to call them in. Somehow they are last on a long list of patients and, as always, I am behind schedule. They do not complain, though Peter does give an occasional anxious look at his watch, knowing it is now dark, there is snow, and the drive home will be difficult.

Anna is eighty-nine-years-old; Peter is ninety-two. They have been married for sixty-six years. Ten years ago, Anna had a heart attack complicated by some congestive heart failure, and it was my privilege to become one of her physicians. Her cardiac status has been relatively stable over the years, requiring at most some small adjustment in medication from time to time; but now she also has developed advanced Alzheimer's disease.

Peter has always come with her, even back years ago during the good times. He checks on her prescriptions, explains her medical history, and occasionally mentions an ache or pain of his own in an off-hand manner, needing only a nod of reassurance from me. He is in charge.

About six years ago, I began to hear jokes between them about Anna's memory. She'd forget a name or a phone number, lose a necklace, or misplace her glasses. At first all these little things seemed funny to them and were perceived as part of getting older. But the little things kept multiplying and loomed larger and larger as a slow but inexorable process seemed to eat away at the Anna we knew, leaving an empty, pitiful, helpless shell.

A neurological evaluation of Anna resulted in a diagnosis of Alzheimer's disease, and since then the deterioration has been relentless, terrifying. She often does not even recognize Peter, and when she is spoken to can only giggle hopelessly, without understanding or purpose. She has lost control of her bladder and bowels, making it necessary for her bed to be protected and for diapers to be put on her throughout the day. It is as if this wonderful, mature woman has returned to infancy, to total dependency.

Peter dresses Anna. He changes her, cleans up after her, and bathes her. Peter speaks to her and for her as one would a young child. This gaunt, weak, arthritic old man cares for his wife with pride, tenderness, and without apology. Their children try to convince him to have Anna put in a nursing home, but he refuses, seeming to gain new strength and purpose in his unsought but unshirked task. Caring for Anna has become Peter's whole life.

Peter has found a restaurant near their home where he feels comfortable, where no one stares or laughs, where he and Anna are known. The owner is a friend who understands. Peter has to spoon-feed Anna most of her meal, which she enjoys with smiles and laughter. In their early years together, Peter and Anna fed, changed, and bathed their infant children together, proud of what their love had wrought, hopeful of a future bright with dreams. But now Anna is the child.

Peter tells me about the last few months with Anna. It's

worse now than before, much worse. She does not recognize him most of the time and won't take the medicine she is supposed to.

When he tried to get her ready to come for this office visit, she resisted being dressed and soiled her clothes once more. The visits with me have become more and more an opportunity for Peter to share his story, his trouble, his despair. "Everything is all right," I reassure him. "You're doing a great job of taking care of her, Peter."

This visit takes a long time. Peter has a lot on his mind. I feel depressed and helpless myself, because I am unable to offer any suggestion that might improve their plight. Finally they get up to go. We help Anna back on with her dress and coat, then into the wheelchair. Peter reaches into his coat pocket and pulls out a ruffled piece of cardboard. For a moment, time stops. Peter trembles; I feel uncertain what is happening.

For what seems an interminable minute, Peter and I communicate in silence, searching one another's eyes, feeling more than either of us can verbalize. I understand his fatigue, his weariness, his despair; but I also know the strength from within that comes from his faith. He holds on to a hope that is *their* hope, persists in a love that is *their* love.

Peter turns toward Anna, looking for the life-partner who is no longer present. Her eyes are vacant and she giggles unaware. Finally, Peter comes out with the words, his voice weak and yet determined. "Anna and I want you to accept this gift for Christmas," he declares. "We want you to know how much we appreciate your time and concern." He hands me the piece of cardboard, a cereal box-top with a bracelet stuck to it with masking tape. Awkwardly, he apologizes for having wrapped the gift so plainly.

The stones on the bracelet had been found by the two of them on a vacation trip to Arizona years ago. Peter had made the bracelet at home. He had ground and rubbed each stone, making them shine as if they were rubies, then glued each into its setting with care.

No greater gift have I ever received. It is the gift of the Magi. It is the gift of love.

TWELVE

TWO FUNERALS

I have attended two funerals this week, one large, one small. Alzheimer's disease was directly or indirectly responsible for both deaths, and thus connects them in my mind.

Barbara's nursery school was a beginning for so many. She was a mother to all the kids, a sister to their young mothers, a listener to their fathers, a friend to everyone. Barbara's door was always as open as her heart. She gave naturally. She loved naturally. Her life was snuffed out suddenly at age fifty-four in a tragic automobile accident. There was no warning, no time for fear, no chance for pain. They say the driver of the other car had Alzheimer's.

Barbara's funeral was an occasion—the large church filled, the entire community present to pay tribute that was earned, earnest, and regal. There was a choir with soloist and a grand procession of grieving family that brought tears to all of our eyes. As at any time of tragedy, the hundreds of friends felt a desperate need to do something—anything—to help. And since there was really little that could be done, we all did what people always do: we cooked. There was more food at Barbara's funeral luncheon than the gathering could possibly eat. The community met as one to honor a great lady and to remember her many gifts of love.

Anna's end, in contrast, had come slowly and painfully at age ninety-three after years of embarrassing deterioration due to her Alzheimer's. No longer able to care for herself, express herself, or even remember her husband Peter's name, she had become as helpless as a child. Peter bathed her, fed her, dressed her, cleaned up after her. He is now ninety-six, but his devotion to Anna has kept him strong through all the years of her illness. I watched this love story in awe, knowing that it was extraordinary and of God.

Anna's funeral was obscure, small, quiet. A few family members were there, relieved that their long ordeal was finally over. And Peter, finally allowing himself to be vulnerable, cried out for his beloved wife, upset that she hadn't been made to appear in death as she had to him in life—still the beautiful young girl he'd married seventy years before. Peter's reason for being was now gone; he felt that his life was over, too. He sat alone and weakly greeted the few people who visited the small, near-empty chapel.

Peter broke into tears when I came to view Anna's body and to hug the man I'd come to respect so much. As a doctor, I had not been able to change the course of Anna's disease. I had only had the privilege of listening to and marveling at their story of love so great.

Two funerals, two different stories . . . connected by Alzheimer's and love.

THIRTEEN

MARTHA

Martha sits in the family waiting room outside of the coronary care unit. She has been married fifty-seven years to Chester, who now lies in limbo on a respirator, his outcome uncertain, his prognosis guarded. Martha has known for some time that this day would come, but she still struggles against the pain—allowing herself tears but at the same time berating herself for what she sees as her own weakness. I sit down next to her and place my arm around her shoulders, telling her that Chester is holding his own but that there has been no improvement.

"It's truly in God's hands now, Martha," I tell her. "We're doing everything we can. We must both be patient now and wait to see what direction this is going to go. Chester knows you're here."

She grips my hand and starts to cry. "See these rings he gave me?" she asks, holding out her left hand. "That's the one he gave me for our wedding, and that other one with the five diamonds is the one he gave me on our fiftieth wedding anniversary. I just can't let him go, but I've got to accept this, don't I?"

My own thoughts race and search for the words of comfort that usually wind up coming from somewhere outside of me. I simply hold her tightly, letting her talk because she needs to and allowing my voice to echo the mantra of all physicians: "You are not alone. Don't be too hard on yourself. There is nothing more you can do. Chester is fighting hard and so are we. We all just need some time now. Your husband can't speak to you because of his respirator, but he knows you're here and feels your love."

Then I squeeze her hand more tightly and listen more carefully, for between her sobs there is an anguish that needs to speak: "I know he's fighting against that machine, Doctor. The nurses told me that when he does that, it's hard for them to keep his breathing right." She pauses and shudders, grasping for control. "But I just don't know what that fighting is all about. He might be telling us to stop. What if he's ready to let go? Is that why he's fighting like that? Maybe he's ready, but I just can't let him go." Then she pauses again and another gush of warm tears causes her to reach into her purse for a handkerchief. "Isn't that dumb? Why can't I just accept it?"

My own thought processes shift forward at this point. For I myself was still holding out a reasonable hope for Chester's surviving this episode. I had not intended to discuss the issue of how long to prolong his life-support systems today, yet as I listen it becomes clear that Martha needs to address them.

"You know, Doctor," she explains, "a month ago Chester told me we should go out and choose cemetery plots, and I just wouldn't let him do that. He told me never to put him in a nursing home or let him become a vegetable.

"I have this funny feeling when I go home now. Chester's always been there, you know. I just can't get used to his not being there. That first night he came in? Before he was on the machine? He asked me where I'd slept and I told him the middle bedroom. I told him the heat was better there, but that wasn't really the reason. I lied. I tried to sleep in our bedroom, but without him there I just couldn't do it. Every night for fifty-seven years, I've cuddled up next to him to go to sleep, and now . . . ." Martha collapses again into tears and all I can do is hold her.

After a few long moments of silence, I asked whether her daughter would be coming today to be with her. "Oh, Mona was here yesterday," she says. "But she has to sing in the choir at church this morning. They really need her. Chester would want her to do that, too. She'll be back tomorrow.

"The grandkids all want me to put up the Christmas decorations but I just can't. I don't feel it's right without Chester. The Christmas tree means everything to him. He was poor when he grew up. There were eight kids in his family and the tree was all they ever had for Christmas. I don't feel right putting ours up without Chester. Isn't that dumb? I've just got to accept his not being there, but I can't. It isn't Christmas without him. I'm sorry for all this, Doctor. I'm taking so much of your time!"

I ask Martha if she'd like to go in with me to see Chester and she agrees. But I warn her again that he has had sedatives and will not respond to her this morning. At the bedside she gamely steps to his side and takes his hand, then starts to gently caress his brow.

"It's okay, honey," she says. "I'm here. Everything is going to be all right. You hear? Just be quiet and rest, dear. I love you. I'll be back in a while. You just rest." She turns to leave the room and we walk out hand in hand to the hall. Words are not necessary.

CODA

The following morning Chester is still showing no signs of improvement. I seek out Martha again after rounds. "Martha," I say, "things look about the same today. Not really much improvement. We are doing what we can."

She responds quickly and in more control than yesterday. "I can see that, Doctor. He wouldn't want us to leave him like this. I just know."

I reply: "Yesterday's conversation got me thinking a lot, Martha. I still can't tell what direction this thing is going to go; but if God decides to take Chester by stopping his heart or something, then I think it would probably be best not to try to revive him."

"I agree completely," she declares. "Please don't do anything extraordinary to prolong Chester's life. I'm afraid we've done too much already. He told me he was going to die and I didn't believe him. Guess that's because I didn't want to."

We have another good hug, and I think we both feel some relief as we both cross that barrier between holding on and letting go. Martha looks me in the eyes and says, "You know, Doctor, I did go home last night and put up the Christmas tree. I put it right where Chester could look at it from his favorite chair. Tonight I'll put the lights on and some decorations. Just in case."

FOURTEEN

KIM

Kim recently suffered a small heart attack and now gets angina if she overexerts. Formal stress tests show that she is rather severely limited for a fifty-one-year old. Kim has a brand new grandson she wants to play with, a garden to tend, and an active social life she wishes to resume. After much discussion of risks and potential benefits, her doctors recommended the balloon angioplasty procedure and referred her to me. This is an entirely appropriate option for Kim. I reviewed her chart and initial diagnostic studies and agreed enthusiastically to undertake the procedure.

When I stop by Kim's hospital room the night prior to the scheduled operation, however, I find that she is still very reluctant and uncertain. Even though she has consented to this treatment course, she is now having second thoughts as she reconsiders the risks. In order to proceed, I of course have to obtain written, informed consent. With serious surgery, fear is always present. The operating physician needs to instill confidence and trust while at the same time providing information on the risks honestly.

Whenever doctors who do not perform surgical procedures talk to patients about having them done, there is unintentionally a lot left out. The doctors are aware of risks and mention them in a very "by-the-way" manner that is often not even heard by the patient. It is not that these doctors are trying to hide anything; it is simply that they do not understand the reality of the risks themselves. Most of them have never had to tell a family that their loved one has died or had a stroke on the operating table. There is no more difficult task in all of medicine.

Only since I started doing angioplasty have I begun to learn this other side—the surgeon's side—of medicine. Only now do I understand the guilt of having hurt someone, the depression that accompanies failure, the humility of knowing I made matters worse rather than better, the loss of self-confidence that accompanies the lonely feeling after an unsuccessful outcome. As an internist, I often failed to save a patient; death is part of medicine and always will be. But for the non-surgeon, it is always the *disease* that kills the patient, not something the doctor did or did not do.

When the outcome of surgery is less than hoped for, however, the surgeon often questions himself or herself: "Did my actions lead directly to this outcome? Was this complication or death my fault? Was I simply not good enough? Should I have done it another way? Maybe I shouldn't have tried the procedure in the first place."

Surgeons often blame themselves for failure, but they must go on, for there are many wonderful successes—patients made better, fear relieved, crises calmed. The emotional high of having actually done something to relieve or stem the tide of disease is one I have known. There is no greater sense of accomplishment or participation in God's healing power.

For a sensitive person, however, this emotional rollercoaster is stressful. It demands new strength and courage, yet at the same time new humility and restraint. Above all, surgery has given me a whole new respect and appreciation for the term "informed consent"—once for me a mere legal paper-passing, a necessary nuisance in the practice of medicine but now a serious, moral issue that I approach in a whole new way.

I suppose that underneath my concern there is a practical knowledge of the legal implications of not obtaining such consent, yet for me it is a much more personal matter. I must be sure that each time I take a risk with a patient he or she and the family not only understand but also agree with the decision and know the real expectations of our imperfect science. Consent is as much for me and my own conscience as for anything else.

Angioplasty is different from most other surgery in one very important respect: the patient is awake during the entire procedure. If a life-threatening complication occurs, therefore, the physician must not only deal with the medical emergency but also with the psychological crisis of a conscious patient who must be rushed off to open-heart surgery. For this type of event to be handled smoothly, there must be preparedness, determination, and understanding on the part of both the doctor and the patient. If adequate time has been spent developing a trusting relationship between the two, then untoward events are simply managed and the outcome—even if less than hoped for—is accepted with a more realistic perspective.

Kim's decision comes with much difficulty. I explain to her the serious aspects of her situation that led to our offering—and recommending—angioplasty. Even though her doctors had gone over the risks with her, our discussion is in much more depth, particularly in relation to the long-term efficacy and surgical risk of the procedure.

Kim reluctantly signs the release form, but I make it clear to her that I do not want to proceed until she is convinced in her own mind about the decision. Leaving the room, I know her uncertainty, her fear, her reluctance is still great. I realize that Kim is not committed, not ready to face her overwhelming fear. After an hour of earnest discussion, I feel Kim is, in fact, "informed," but her "consent" is on paper only. Despite going ahead with plans for the surgery, I am not at ease. Legally, she has elected to have the operation, but emotionally and morally my own feelings about her decision are in turmoil.

CODA

The next morning, I receive a call that Kim has decided to cancel the procedure and go home. This last-minute change in my day's schedule neither surprises nor upsets me, for I know Kim is simply not ready. I stop by her room briefly this time—not to change her mind but to tell her I understand.

Time will tell whether my style of medical practice is best for someone like Kim. But I know it is the only way that I can ever do it.

FIFTEEN

MICHAEL AND EMILY

I am becoming more and more doubtful about the directions new technology has taken us in medicine. Try as I might to keep an open mind to "progress," my heart keeps screaming to me that there is something wrong: wrong goals, wrong motivations, wrong order of priorities, wrong directions.

Michael is forty-one—younger than I am—and dying of congestive heart failure. For several months he has been told that his only chance to survive is to have a cardiac transplantation (heart transplant). When I met Michael a week ago he turned weakly toward me and gazed into my eyes—his shriveled body wasted, his breathing forced, his pitiful expression begging for relief. "If I'm going to die," he said, "please just let me go home. But if I'm still on the list for a transplant, then can't we get on with it?"

Suffering is such a large word. Michael's wife, Emily, is helpless, already knowing in her heart the final outcome, yet outwardly clinging to this last straw of hope put before them. The doctors tell her that modern medicine might keep her husband alive—if he can make it long enough to find a donor heart.

She and her family struggle on, waiting for this promised miracle. Patients like Michael all over the country stay alive—avoiding death, refusing death, disclaiming death—because we doctors tell them to do so.

Michael cannot even make the first team—that list of fellow cardiac sufferers waiting for a heart transplantation. He suffered a pulmonary embolus (a blood clot on the lung) last week that increased his risk in surgery. If we can keep him alive for six more weeks after that event—and nothing else happens—Michael might actually get on the list . . . to wait some more. And for what? Are we relieving his suffering or prolonging it?

Emily is here today, watching her husband's long ordeal with slow death playing out its final scenes, the false hope of transplantation becoming more and more a myth as the reality of his death marches toward an inevitable conclusion. It is my first meeting with her, because I am just starting my rotation on the hospital service. This makes the interview more difficult, but the time has come to face truth, to put aside fantasy, to let God's will be done.

Emily knows in her heart that there will be no magical happy ending. Strong and composed, she listens to my words knowingly, her lips held firmly in an outward appearance of strength but trembling as she fights back her tears.

When the tears finally come, she allows herself to be held in my arms, accepting my shoulder as a momentary refuge. "I just don't know what's in the future," she cries. "Do you know? How long does he have?"

We discuss her husband's stated desire to die at home. I do not speak of "pulling out the plug" nor ask her for a final decision. I just ask this brave woman to start thinking about whether she could take Michael home with her. It is so much to ask—perhaps too much. I tell her God will help us all with the decision, that we must accept death and let it be as beautiful and peaceful as it can be. Once we give our lives up to God, I say, time will show us the way. We need only to "let go and let God."

CODA

Afterwards, I start walking away with Dennis, my resident, at my side. All at once my own emotions surface, causing a swell of tears that need to be released. I have held these back in order to do my job with Michael and Emily the best that I know how.

Sometimes my own tears surprise me, assuring me that God is with me in these moments of facing death. I do what I have to do well, for I allow myself to love my patients and their families, but the pain I feel is still real.

I'm glad Dennis is here to see this. Someday soon he will have to make the hard decisions, and then—only then—will he begin to learn what being a physician is all about. Through my tears, I hope he is learning the truth.

SIXTEEN

GARY AND JEANEEN

Gary is a machinist, forty-two, young in appearance and behavior. I've never been quite sure what a machinist does—an admission that certainly reveals my own sheltered and relatively privileged upbringing. But I do know that Gary works on a line in a factory with long variable shifts, is a member of a union, and has known terminations and lay-offs before. He has had regular work for about a year now, but news of another round of lay-offs has again raised the specter of uncertainty and self-doubt.

Gary's wife, Jeaneen, has more reliable work at a small community hospital, where she is a secretary. Her income is meager, but at least it can be counted on. They have two boys, ten and fourteen. The family's health insurance is paid for by Jeaneen's employer.

When Gary is working, he is proud, self-confident, and full of youthful laughter and good humor. Unemployment, however, is becoming more frequent and more prolonged. When he is out of work, Gary's laughter becomes a nervous, self-conscious giggle, his stride and demeanor tremulous and timid, his voice friendly but unsure. He still loves to talk of hunting season, football, the kids' sporting events, but if the conversation turns even for a moment to his wife's job or their finances, Gary feels emasculated and retreats to a posture of inadequacy that is at the same time both real and imagined.

Gary's brother had bypass surgery three years ago. Now it is Gary's turn to face this challenge in his life. Five days ago he woke with severe pain in his chest and arms, accompanied by endless nausea. In the emergency room, an electrocardiogram was clear-cut: heart attack. We were able to limit the damage to Gary's heart somewhat with new clot-removing drugs (thrombolytics), followed later by angioplasty; but this young man has had a major insult to his heart muscle and will have to be rehabilitated slowly over several months before he can safely return to full activity.

Now comes the hard part. Gary must recover his self-confidence where there is so little to start with. His physical restrictions will only further convince him of his own uselessness. His physicians and rehabilitation team must understand the silent, unstated, unmeasurable emotional pain that far exceeds the physical pain from his heart disease.

On the fourth day of his recovery, Gary seems to have more spirit. His attitude is more positive than it has been the first three days. I complete my routine examination, finding blood pressure, pulse, rhythm all stable. The nurses tell me that he's been flirting with them that morning, so I comment upon it: "Gary, things look good today, I think you're making excellent progress. Today you may spend as much time up in the chair as you like." Then in a kidding tone I add: "But the ladies tell me you've been flirting with them. I don't know if you're ready for that yet!"

Gary's eyes sparkle with life and a big grin emerges from a face that up until now has been quite somber. He replies in a whispering tone: "Doc, I know I'm better this morning. I woke up with an erection! You've sure got a lot of good lookers working here. Makes a man feel like a man; know what I mean?"

I know exactly what Gary means. It is important that my response be encouraging while at the same time appropriate for this relatively young man trying to lift himself up from a knockdown punch. So I keep the tone light: "Hold on big fellow. You're going to have to cool your jets for a few weeks, my friend. That heart of yours needs some time to rest. But don't worry. You'll be back in the saddle before you know it!" Gary gets the message, but his spirits remain resilient.

The remainder of his hospital course is uncomplicated and I am able to discharge him on the tenth day. Jeaneen is quiet but determined on the day he goes home. We concentrate on the subjects of diet, medication regimen, and most importantly his appointments for regular attendance at his rehabilitation exercise program where he will work under supervision to gradually increase his activity.

There are a lot of subjects left untouched at this stage. Jeaneen doesn't have to say anything; her expression tells it all. She has a hundred hidden questions about her family's future: jobs, finances, sex, her own feelings of responsibility for a predicament she feels she needs to control but cannot. Jeaneen is strong-willed and loyal but silently afraid.

CODA

It is now three weeks later. Gary and Jeaneen have returned for their first outpatient visit since his discharge. Gary has been participating in the cardiac rehabilitation program regularly, and physically he is doing well. Life at home is far from normal, though. There is an unstated, undefined, unmeasured, yet deeply felt distance that separates these two spouses.

Gary for his part is reaching out to find and exhibit his manhood: "Doc, there's nothing wrong with—you know—our fooling around now, is there? Tell my wife it's okay."

I look at Jeaneen, whose silence speaks of her ambivalence toward a part of their lives that she considers relatively unimportant at this critical time. She understands Gary's needs and has been willing to cooperate once or twice since discharge; but she feels no passion, only fear. Gary feels this silent barrier between them but believes that his performance in the bedroom will prove to her—and to himself—that he is still a healthy man. They cannot speak of this problem at home, but here in the doctor's office their feelings can be vented. My response has to be generalized and include the needs of both of them.

"You two are beautiful individuals, and I wish I had an instant solution for you," I explain. "I don't, but this is such a common situation after heart attacks that I do get to talk to people about it all the time. So please don't feel embarrassed.

"I'm going to say some things that may or may not apply directly to the two of you; because I cannot possibly know you that well. All I know is that sex is a normal part of married existence and that when one spouse becomes seriously ill there is, for a time, a loss of the spontaneity and naturalness that makes sex the beautiful thing it can be. I can promise that things are going to get better, but it isn't going to happen overnight. It's going to take time.

"Jeaneen, you know that most guys do start to feel pretty upset if they go too long without sex. I know, because I'm a guy, too. Total abstinence can cause frustration and anxiety that can be more harmful than the physical exertion of sex itself. You know there are some positions with the guy on the bottom where he doesn't have to work so hard; for a few months it might be a good idea to try this. And you know what? It's sexy! Try it out when you have intercourse."

Gary breaks into a broad grin, turning to Jeaneen as if to say, 'I told you so!' "That sounds good, Doc," he says enthusiastically. Meanwhile, Jeaneen sits quietly, her eyes demanding more.

I continue: "But Gary, there's a much more important suggestion I have for you that in the long run will make the biggest difference in your lives. Right now Jeaneen is naturally going to be a little reticent about having sex. For one thing, she's afraid you'll over do it; for another, she's got a lot on her mind besides sex. It's important that you understand her feelings in all of this. Lots of times illness is harder on the spouse than on the patient. Be patient. Love each other and talk to each other about your real feelings. It's the hidden secrets and unspoken hurts and fears that get in the way of intimacy."

"That's it, Doc," Gary responds. "Intimacy. It seems like we just don't have enough of that anymore." Jeaneen also hears what I am saying, because for the first time since this conversation started she leans back, relaxes, and begins to nod her head.

As Gary and Jeaneen leave the office and walk down the hall, I watch as Jeaneen reaches out and grabs Gary's hand. They look at each other for a moment and get on the elevator, hand-in-hand.

SEVENTEEN

VERONICA

Veronica comes from the hospital room choking back still another tear, miming with her hands an invisible piece of paper. "I just think I should have something before I leave that tells me I don't have a husband anymore. He's . . . gone."

She uses a handkerchief to wipe the wetness from her eyes and then grabs my arm one last time. "Thank you," she whispers in a gravelly voice different from just a few moments ago. Then, thrusting the handkerchief away into her pocket for later, she turns and walks bravely away, her daughters and their husbands trailing behind.

The ordeal has gone on for weeks, far too many weeks. Veronica has endured daily visits to this hospital where Frank, her husband of forty-five years, lay dying—suspended between non-life and non-death. Heart surgery had been Frank's only hope, a risk worth taking, for heart disease had turned the man Veronica loved into a crippled, despondent, suffering, fearful ghost of what he had been before. We doctors had felt there was a chance, and this was true; but after the operation, one complication after another nibbled away at that chance—devouring the hope, slowly draining the last glass of wine.

A mechanical respirator kept Frank's body alive, but there was only coma—endless coma—in his future. The course was done; the time had come to bring the tragedy of death prolonged, pain endured, end postponed to a close. For nearly three months Veronica's family had been living in limbo, aware in their hearts that Frank would not—could not—return. Like all of us, they needed someone to lift that burden from them.

Again as a physician I found a special moment in not doing rather than in doing; in simply allowing the beauty, the peace, the mystery of death to bring a family closer together in love. We talked and I felt their pain. Frank was not going to come home. The respirator was only prolonging his death, not giving him life. The time had come for the family to gather, to touch Frank, to hug him, to say their goodbyes. Then the machine had to be removed.

I told Veronica I would stay by their side until the end. I did not know how long it would take, and Frank actually breathed on his own for several hours after the machine was disconnected. He was peaceful, with arms folded in a cross over his chest, breathing but not struggling. The room was strangely quiet with curtains drawn, yet I felt a presence there with us. I needed that presence to keep me strong and assure me that this was the right thing to do.

Now Veronica and her family, even in their grief, thank me over and over again. Their praise makes me feel uncomfortable, yet after my own emotional turmoil it is almost as if God is telling me, "It's all right, John."

EIGHTEEN

WILLIAM

William is a college-level physical education instructor who has always been extremely health-conscious and, if anything, overly concerned about his own condition. He has a congenital heart valve abnormality that finally led a year or two ago to surgical replacement at age fifty-five.

It is unfortunate that some individuals require an artificial heart valve, because the valve makes noise. It sounds like a loud antique clock, constantly reminding the patient of time passing, of death faced, of a vulnerability it is best to ignore. Click, click, click . . . the valve's cadence is an ever-present reminder of frailty, mortality, weakness.

William has actually done beautifully since his operation, still exercises daily, jogs, and stays active. He reads everything he can get his hands on about the heart, new developments, and risk factors. But he's the kind of guy you hate to see on your outpatient list, because he has so many questions about little details that he has built up in his mind as being immediate threats. Every question William asks could be given an answer that would magnify his fear, and thus I handle him with reassuring generalities which are enough to satisfy an intelligent man yet put in terms that ease his tension and allay his fear.

Today he asks about his risk of developing AIDS from the transfusions he has had, and—though his coronary arteries were normal at the time of surgery—he wants to know whether there is any chance they "could" block up. (This is like asking if he could die in an automobile accident if he drives to New York.) William's whole being is centered around the risk of death, to the point where his very living is limited because of his fear.

William understands that he is this way. I have had numerous frank discussions with him about health consciousness which hinders rather than helps, stifles rather than avoids, interferes with rather than enhances his ability to enjoy what he has.

I cannot change who William is. I can only serve as a sounding board for him and hope that my answers relieve some of his imagined threat. On each visit William's eyes have a frightened look of expectancy, concentration, and fear. His hands are held taut, as if he is clinging to a cliff. The fear in the room is not just verbalized; it is visible, touchable, recognizable in every strained movement and every question that he has carefully prepared during his sleepless nights at home. Aware of every heartbeat, afraid of every blood test, William lives concerned that there may be no tomorrow . . . while another today of living slips away.

CODA

As I am returning to my office after evening rounds a few months later, I find William wandering aimlessly around the hospital hallway. He is not waiting for an appointment nor to complain of any new ailment—just wandering late at night in an empty corridor. I am tired and have in my own mind finished my day, so at first I am mildly irritated to be delayed on my way home to rest and family. However, I keep these thoughts to myself and ask William if I can be of any help.

"No, thanks, Doctor. Everything is going all right. I've been feeling fine. Don't worry, I'm doing okay," William insists. His words are reassuring, but his manner is not. There is a trembling in his voice, an uncertainty in his step, an aura of fear that betrays his words. Something is wrong. Something has brought William to this place at this unusual hour, and it is creating a monstrous upheaval of emotion in this man I know so well. Yet William seems reluctant to tell, hesitant to confide—as if I shouldn't be bothered. So I push a little. With an arm placed on his shoulder, I ask again what brought him to the hospital. His eyes well with tears; his body shakes. He is clearly afraid to ask for help, ashamed to need it, uncertain, lost, and confused.

But still he resists. "You needn't be concerned, Doctor," he says. "It is not your problem. It's my dad. He has cancer and may be dying tonight downstairs. I'm here because of him. I don't know what might happen. The doctors say he could die at any time. They've done all they can do. It's just a matter of time. I don't know whether to go home or not." William's tears come closer to the surface; his agony becomes more obvious, his pain more clear.

I give him a hug and talk a little bit about my own dad and my own feelings when he died. I ask William if he has simply told his dad he loves him. He hesitates, stuttering an incomplete sentence that indicates he has not: "I don't know if . . . ."

I tell him he must go now, tonight, to his father's bedside, kneel down and hug him as tightly as he can, look deep into his father's eyes and simply say, "I love you."

So William goes and hugs his dad, tells him of his love, and thanks him for all there is to thank a father for. Not many hours later, his father dies.

William will never forget that he grasped his opportunity; nor will I forget that I took those few extra minutes with a patient who needed me.

NINETEEN

HELEN

Yesterday was hard, cold, painful. Yesterday was wasted, exhausting, futile. The taste is still bitter, the air still stagnant, my eyes still reddened, my gait still hesitant, my voice still muffled as I try to recall the events.

My personal friend Helen—also a physician—has herself been ill. She is dying slowly of cancer, yet is facing her fate with an inner strength and faith that touches everyone around her and teaches us the meaning of courage.

Helen's mother had been hospitalized recently for congestive heart failure but seemed to have been getting better. Helen had gone ahead reluctantly with vacation plans with her family, urged to do so by her mother. Then suddenly, quietly, Helen's mother slipped away, dying in her sleep. It fell to me to interrupt the long-awaited family vacation with this terrible news by telephone. Now Helen wishes she had not left, and I feel responsible, thinking somehow I could have done something to avoid giving my friend such pain.

Yesterday I watched as Helen's father said goodbye to his lifelong partner. Afraid, alone, he touched the body from which he took life, to which he gave life, and with which he created life.

Tears came during fleeting relaxations of his taut facial muscles, each time with an apology—as if tears were somehow not allowed or unmanly. They finally gushed forth in a torrent when I reassured him that he must release his grief and allow his love to be expressed. I cried too—for him, for Helen, and for myself as well.

Now as the hours stand still, I begin to slide backwards into a cloud of uncertainty and self-doubt—the inevitable second-guessing of the physician who has lost a patient and feels that he or she has failed, that death might have been averted, that his or her actions might have changed time, controlled life.

These are not unique feelings. All of us tend to search for someone or something to blame when a person dies. Loving family members do so, and doctors do so as well. We must do this, because the alternative is to accept the utterly inevitable, unchangeable, uncontrollable limits of our own mortality. We want to be in control, but to accept death means we must release control.

This time is more difficult than most for me, however. For as often as I have glimpsed the unknowable door of death with patients in the past and as often as I have shed tears with the living, there has always been a certainty that I had done my duty. This time there is a friend involved whose life already has been racked by suffering, whose life has been lived under the shadow of death for years. This time it was Helen's mom. I wanted so much to spare her this pain.

TWENTY

PHILIP AND ROSE

Philip had long had chronic kidney failure, treated by my friend and neighbor, Dr. Brown, with his usual wisdom, grace, and cautious observation. Philip realized it was only a matter of time before chronic dialysis would have to be initiated, but this vigorous, kind and independent seventy-year-old knew full well that this would mean becoming dependent on a machine. He resisted such treatment until absolutely necessary, knowing that with the machine would come the private agony of loss of freedom and confidence that any medical dependence brings.

Then coronary artery disease entered to complicate Philip's life, a life that was already in the shadow of chronic illness. Medicines eased his angina at first, but a relentless progression of his cardiac symptoms kept him from his gardening, from walking . . . in fact, from living. Each pain brought with it a deep, terrifying, irrepressible sense of doom. Confined, restricted, afraid to do the slightest task lest it waken the monster pain inside, Philip brooded—unhappy yet undaunted. He refused to accept life as it has become.

Philip told Dr. Brown that he was ready to undertake any risk if there is a chance of alleviating his pain, that he would rather die than continue suffering to such a degree. A cardiac catheterization demonstrated severe blockages in all of Philip's major coronary arteries—clearly the cause of his pain. This left Philip with only two choices: bypass surgery or angioplasty.

I was consulted to help decide the best course of action for Philip, because angioplasty is in my area of special interest. One of the many nice things about working in a large group practice is the ability to have immediate access to consultation with other doctors whom one knows and trusts. Dr. Brown and I called in one of our heart surgeons, and the three of us sat down together with all the data in front of us. There would be no easy answers—of that much we were certain. We would have to go one way or the other in order to relieve Philip's suffering, and there would be no cure. Our goal was only to alleviate the pain. As a team, we knew surgery of any kind was running a high risk, but Philip had left us no choice. He understood that risk and wanted us to try something.

Under normal circumstances, bypass surgery would have been considered, but this was no ordinary situation. The process of going on a heart-lung machine during the surgery would have stressed Philip's kidneys to such a degree that his already tenuous kidney function would almost certainly have deteriorated. Chronic dialysis would then be immediately necessary—an outcome Philip wanted to avoid if there was any possibility at all of fixing his heart another way.

I thought that angioplasty offered palliation and at the same time a better chance for his staying off dialysis. This solution was reasonable, logical, but still risky. The entire team settled on this carefully thought out alternative plan, one which we all knew was a compromise based on Philip's unique situation. I agreed to undertake the procedure as long as Philip understood the limitations and risks.

On the evening prior to performing the procedure, I sat with Philip in his hospital room. It was then that I came to know him as a human being. He told me that he had been raised in the house just across the street from my present home and related wonderful stories of those days when he was just a boy and would come over to what is now my backyard and climb the big apple tree behind the house with his friends. Philip loved that big tree; he would pick apples and eat one after another on those carefree, lazy summer days of his youth.

I told Philip that my family and I had just lost that big old wonderful tree with its shade for the deck and its tire swing for the kids. We lost it in a storm; its huge trunks had been rotted on the inside. On the morning the tree surgeons were to come and cut away the fallen tree, my then seven-year-old daughter, Emily, sat out back on the deck to have one last breakfast with her friend the tree, giving one of its remaining boughs a hug before she got on her bike to leave for school. Our whole family was saddened by that loss, and so now was Philip.

The next morning, however, Philip and I were in good spirits as we started. Both of us felt good about our discussion the night before. Patients are awake during angioplasty, and Philip actually chattered away with more apple tree stories as I was inserting the catheters in his groin and preparing the equipment. He was trying to tell everyone in the operating room how he once fell out of the tree, but he was rambling somewhat incoherently under the influence of the valium, the mild sedative we administer prior to any procedure of this type.

Early on during the angioplasty, I thought we had beaten the odds. The procedure started well, the tiny wire and balloon catheter slipping easily down to the first of the blockages, opening it successfully.

I then moved on to the next site of blockage in one of the larger arteries. At first, the initial response at this second site was good also. But then suddenly, unexpectedly, the miracle of success turned into the agony of failure as this large artery went into spasm and closed upon itself. Despite every possible effort, we were not able to reverse the catastrophic event. There followed immediate shock. Philip's blood pressure collapsed and would not respond to any of our efforts. Then came death . . . and silence.

As the course of events turned against Philip, we paged Dr. Brown and he dropped what he was doing and came immediately to help out with his long-time patient. But there was nothing any of us could do. At the end, Dr. Brown went to the waiting room himself to tell Philip's wife, Rose, that he had died. By the time I finished up and went to see her myself, I found that she had left.

Intellectually, rationally, practically, I knew that I had done my best, that the decision process had been proper, that as a physician I had performed well. Emotionally, however, I was torn by feelings of failure, self-doubt, and grief.

Tormented by the knowledge that under my care a man had died, I knew that before I could turn to the solace, the salve, the healing of sleep that night, I must first be allowed to console the patient's wife. Yet she had left the hospital in despair, gone home with her tears to her family.

Never before have I felt so utterly alone and incomplete.

CODA

Philip and Rose's home is in town, the address easy to find. I see vividly every crack in the sidewalk, every picket gate, every neighbor's door as I walk from my car to their house. Trembling with fear and guilt, I—the failure, the outsider, the villain—knock on the door, fully expecting in my imaginings that I will be scorned, rebuked, disdained. Yet when the door is opened by a family member, I am welcomed into the home with love, respect, grace, and understanding. Those gathered there seem surprised at my grief but recognize the intensity of my feelings and my need to speak with Philip's widow.

Rose comes toward me with arms outstretched, tears without shame, love without blame. We hug each other tightly for what seems like a day. Then sitting on the couch and holding Rose's hands, I recount the events, explaining as well as I can the reasons for our failure. I tell her that Philip had become unconscious very shortly after the spasm in the artery and that he had therefore experienced very little pain. She tells me that she had had a premonition from the beginning that Philip would die. Neither of us express second thoughts. Though relative strangers, we share a moment of love never to be forgotten.

I leave and walk slowly to my car, alone with my thoughts and prayers. I am tired yet renewed, another day older, yet anxious for tomorrow. Once again, in death life has shown me its true face. I feel a presence with me: unreachable, unfathomable . . . yet very close. God is in me.

The logs cut from the old apple tree are still in back of our house. My family burns the wood in our fireplace from time to time in the winter months, saving it for special times. Each piece is brought into the house with reverence, and we watch the fire in silence—remembering the past, yet warmed by a new flame. Tonight, the smoke rises from our chimney and drifts away as I remember a little boy who once climbed that tree and ate its apples.

TWENTY-ONE

SARAH

Sarah's family was coming for Christmas, and there were many things to do: gifts to buy, food to prepare, a house to decorate. She left for work high spirited and full of plans for the afternoon, readying herself for the holiday season. There was no warning at all of what this day would bring to this vibrant, fifty-three-year-old woman.

The heart attack struck as she was driving, forcing Sarah to pull to the side of the road. Her pain was mostly in her throat, the nausea deep, endless, frightening, offering no relief. Sarah had no choice but to drive herself to the local hospital. The doctors there recognized immediately that Sarah's heart was failing. Stabilizing her the best they could, they called our life flight center fifty miles away for help.

We dispatch one of our special rescue helicopters to retrieve Sarah and now our team of specialists prepare to receive her. Communication is vital at this stage of an emergency. We keep in touch with the nurses in the aircraft by radio, but their attempts to reverse the process of heart failure with drugs fails. Aware only that something terrible has occurred, Sarah is strapped onto a mobile stretcher with intravenous lines running to help sustain her life and flown to us for one last attempt to save her life. If we can open the blocked artery in time we might be able to salvage enough heart muscle to enable Sarah's life functions to survive.

By the time we meet the aircraft and assist in transporting her to the catheterization laboratory, however, we are well over three hours into the heart attack. Most experimental evidence suggests that reopening the blocked blood vessels up to four hours after such an event might save some portion of the damaged heart, and so we work very quickly.

Sarah is pale, frightened, silent—stoically accepting her persistent pain, yet alert and hopeful. I lean over the stretcher and whisper to her that God is holding my hands. She tightens her grasp of my hand and seems comforted. I myself gain courage from my own prayer, even though as I move my focus from her pleading eyes to the monitors I see the falling blood pressure and know the odds are stacking up against us.

Slow, steady, unyielding, unbending, irrepressible shock overtakes Sarah. But there is still a moment of hope. We insert a catheter quickly into her groin and pass it up to her heart, guiding it by the fluoroscope to the suspected artery. With one brief injection of dye, we identify the total blockage of a large coronary artery on the front of her heart. We then pass a tiny wire through the area of clot, and over this wire we slide a balloon catheter out to the site of the occlusion. Without a moment's hesitation, we inflate the balloon, and after a long, uncertain minute we deflate it again to inspect the result.

The artery has opened! There is a restored blood flow into Sarah's damaged, oxygen-starved heart. There is a moment of elation and a rekindling of hope as a caring, dedicated team of professionals feel for a fleeting moment the thrill of success.

But victory over death is not to be ours this day. The gloomy silence of despair soon envelopes all of us. We wait and hope for Sarah to stabilize, but it is too late. Her heart muscle has been too irreversibly damaged to regain any effective pumping action, and we all stand helpless as her blood pressure continues to fall even after our efforts.

CPR (cardiopulmonary resuscitation) is initiated, and while one of my technologists pumps on Sarah's chest to maintain circulation, we shoot one final picture of her heart. The artery we fixed is still open—Sarah is dying despite the success of our efforts. There simply is not enough heart function left to maintain her life. No operation, no machine, no medicine can reverse the course now. I know we have done all that we can do and that it is not enough. Sarah will die.

Most patients at this stage of cardiogenic shock have long-since become unconscious. Sarah has been put on a respirator to help her breathe, so the tube in her throat prevents her from speaking. But Sarah speaks with her eyes. Kept alive by the physical pounding on her chest, she mysteriously remains awake, staring at her helpless heroes, responding to our queries with nods of her head. Calmly now, she seems to understand that death is near.

I wait with only one last hope—that her family will arrive in time to say goodbye. Sending a nurse out to watch for them and bring them immediately to the operating room, our whole focus changes now. We know we cannot save her, but we can do our best to make her death peaceful. I direct my team with arm motions only. The room is deathly silent. Words are unnecessary. Two of the technologists and one of my residents take turns with the CPR. Each time they make a changeover, Sarah drifts briefly off as if to sleep, but she awakens as soon as the pumping restarts. Our hands are now functioning as her heart.

The family does not arrive, and finally I lean over again to speak to Sarah. With tears welling up in my eyes, I tell her that it is over, that we must let her go. I ask if she is ready now. She remains incredibly awake, searching my eyes as I search hers. She nods that she understands—not fighting, not crying, but gently accepting her imminent end with a valor I have never known. Wordlessly, I call off the person who is doing the CPR.

Death does not come soon. The electrocardiogram continues to show activity for nearly fifteen minutes after we stop. Sarah is gone, but we all wait respectfully until the final electrical impulses slow and then finally cease. There is not a sound in the room as we wait for Sarah's death, each of us alone with our own thoughts and prayers. There is more than death here today; there is love.

CODA

Sarah's family arrives about an hour later. They regret that they had not been in time to see her one last time to tell her of their love. I wish they could have seen her death as well, for they would have observed more than terror, more than fear, more than pain. They would have also experienced Sarah's dying peace and the quiet wonder that touched us all at her end.

TWENTY-TWO

HAROLD AND ELLEN

Harold has been a patient of mine for over ten years. A seventy-three-year-old veteran of World War II, Harold is proud to wear his VFW cap and tell stories of the war. Ravaged now by chronic lung and heart disease, he has been a complete invalid for several years, somehow managing to survive medical crisis after crisis, at least two of which were so critical that he had been given up for lost. The old warrior keeps struggling back, but now lives in a steady state of dependency on his good wife, Ellen.

She has understood for years that the medical profession has no more to offer, that Harold will die someday of his heart disease, that she will be alone. Radical—yet pointless—surgery has been considered but appropriately rejected as an option because the risk of death would be unacceptably high. Harold and Ellen understand that it is better to make the most of what they have and accept Harold's symptoms and restrictions than to deny or defy them.

Chronic illness, once accepted, may allow for years of reasonable happiness within the boundaries that the illness sets. Such has been the case with Harold. Despite a setback every year or so requiring hospitalization, Harold is still with us—with all the feelings, instincts, and memories of a proud soldier.

This week, however, the tables have been turned unexpectedly in Harold's life. His wife Ellen, upon whom he has become so dependent, has developed a frightening syndrome of chest pain herself, which immediately raises the fear of possible heart disease in her. After a consultation with her own physician and preliminary testing on a treadmill, which was inconclusive, Ellen was advised to have a heart catheterization. Because of our longstanding relationship, she and Harold asked that I perform the procedure.

Prior to Ellen's scheduled procedure, one of my nurses, who has been with me long enough to know many of my patients and their families, comes down the hall to tell me that there is something "different" about Harold today. He looks "better" somehow. So even though I am seeing his wife in the examination room, I go to the waiting room and say hello to my old patient.

It is as if the man had been transformed. The Harold I knew before was usually slumped over, slow of pace, mired in his dependency on others; this new Harold hops up from his chair and strides over with a confident, upright posture. He is wearing his VFW cap with its many medals. His voice is sure and healthy as he greets me.

"Doc," he says enthusiastically, "it's my turn now! She's been looking after me for all these years and now she needs me. I can do it." Then he takes my arm and draws me up close as if to whisper in my ear. "Don't tell her, Doc," he pleads, "but I am still having a lot of pain. But that doesn't matter. I have to be strong now—for her."

The old soldier has been called to arms. Duty, pride, honor, and love lifted him out of his chronic illness and dependency. His symptoms are still present, but his self-pity and fear have been set aside. Harold can now cope with his own pain because someone he loves needs him. It is a perfect case of mind over matter.

Harold truly does look better and feel better. His illness has been put into proper perspective and his overall state of health has been stripped bare of the emotional overtones that too often dominate serious illness. He has exactly the same degree of medical disability that he had two months ago; but a visible, palpable, very real "healing" has occurred because he has mentally dedicated himself to his beloved wife.

Harold has not thought this through philosophically. He did not read any books, recite any prayers, or light any candles. I'm not sure he practices any religion. It does not matter. From deep inside his soul, a spiritual strength has emerged that has been hidden. He has been made whole by his faith in himself and his love of Ellen.

The heart catheterization shows that Ellen fortunately does not have any significant heart disease. Her symptoms had been real, but fear has made them seem more serious than they really are. I am able to relieve her of that fear by reassuring her, but now what of Harold? Will he revert immediately to his emotional state of dependency? Or can I somehow show him the door to faith and self-reliance that he himself has opened—and help him walk through that door to freedom?

The strength one needs to live with and rise above a serious illness is already within us, and that spirit is of God. It is of no consequence at all by what name or means one finds and accepts this truth.

CODA

Several months after that episode, Ellen calls me at home to tell me that Harold had died while out hunting. She says she just wanted me to know and that she is having a pretty rough time right now. "He kissed me good bye that morning, Doc," she sobs, "and somehow I knew—I just knew—he wasn't going to return. He had always told me that's how he wanted to die: out in the woods, doing what he loved to do."

I choke up a little on the phone, and Ellen senses it as if we were in the same room. "He loved you, Doc," she assures me, "you and the others. You kept him alive so he could die his way. You know, the day before deer season, he went out and did some target practice. He hit the bull's-eye dead center. Later, he asked me if I wanted to go with him the next day. I told him I didn't even want him to *see* a deer, because I knew the adrenaline surge would get him. But he just laughed it off and said he wasn't afraid."

I try then to express my sorrow, but I also console Ellen by assuring her that this is how Harold would have wanted it: not death in a hospital bed, pitied and helpless, but death as a vibrant being experiencing life until his last exultant moment of glory. Harold did get his deer—a six point buck! They found it lying still fifty yards away from his body. He had made a perfect final shot, although the excitement probably did in fact take his own life as well. Harold had died gloriously—as he had dreamed he might go.

"You know, Doc," Ellen insists, "I know it happened so quickly that he couldn't have had any pain. Know how I know? Because he hadn't gotten his medicine out. He was just slumped back on the tree trunk with his gun slung across his arms. He looked peaceful, almost like he had a smile on his face. Can you believe he even got the deer?"

Then there is a long pause, and finally Ellen says, "I'm going to miss him a lot Doctor. I've been worrying about Harold dying for the past ten years; it's all I've thought about. I don't know what I'm going to do now that it has really happened."

I tell Ellen I wish I had known so I could have come to the funeral. "Oh," she exclaims, "I didn't want to bother you during the week. I know how busy you are. But I did what Harold wanted right up to the end: he wanted a military funeral, so he got one."

Tears well up in my eyes again as we hang up. I will miss Harold, too, but these are tears of happiness. For I cannot imagine a more perfect ending, a more perfect death for this old warrior. It was his final victory.

AFTERWORD

There is but one message I wish to communicate in these pages: facing death requires the acceptance of God's control in our lives. To deal with serious illness, one must first reach some relationship with God, be it in accordance with organized religion or not.

In relating these stories, I do not presume nor wish to suggest that I—or my patients or their loved ones—have found the only way or that the faith we have discovered is any greater or deeper than the next person's. "Letting go and letting God" is a universal concept requiring only that a greater power in our lives be recognized and trusted.

Our search for meaning in the face of death can be likened to our trying to find the way out of a great forest in which we are lost. We will never get out of the forest, for it is endless. Yet we can become comfortable within its boundless maze if we accept ourselves as being a part of the forest and walk a path that is freely chosen.

My own route has been as circuitous as anyone's. There have been many wrong turns that have led me into impassable thickets, and I have had to retrace my steps until I could try another trail. But I know by the footprints and broken branches I have encountered that others have traversed the path before me.

I do not pretend to know many details about all of the world's religions. I do know that I see religion and faith as two separate things. Religion is a path; faith the goal. All paths can lead to the same inner peace, the same healing, and the same freedom from fear.

May God bless you on your path. Perhaps we shall meet along the way.

ABOUT THE AUTHOR

Dr. John Chapman is a cardiologist on the staff of the Geisinger Medical Center in Danville, Pennsylvania, and a clinical professor of medicine at Jefferson Medical College of Philadelphia. He is a graduate of Colgate University and the University of Virginia School of Medicine. Dr. Chapman is a fellow in the American College of Physicians and the American College of Cardiology. He lives with his wife, Molly, and their two daughters, Emily and Erin. The Chapman family vacations annually in Cape Cod, Massachusetts.

OTHER RESOURCES FROM ACTA PUBLICATIONS

Our Special Pages: A Collection of Poems and Essays Written by Cancer Survivors by the Northeast Regional Cancer Institute. Heroic first-person accounts of battling and conquering this dreaded illness. Fifty-one stories offer spiritual guidance, practical advice about treatments and side-effects, and helpful tips for daily living with cancer. (140 pages, $12.95)

From Grief to Grace: Images for Overcoming Sadness and Loss by Helen Reichert Lambin. This unique, gentle book addresses the powerful emotions common to all experiences of grief. Each of the ten chapters suggests several images—some religious and some secular—to assist people in naming, processing, and overcoming their grief. (84 pages, $8.95)

The New Day Journal: A Journey from Grief to Healing by Sr. Mauryeen O'Brien, O.P. A book offering those who have lost a loved one a structured way to work through the "tasks of grief," including accepting the reality of the loss, experiencing the pain of grief, adjusting to the new environment in which the deceased is missing, and moving on with life. (92 page workbook, $8.95)

The Death of a Husband: Reflections for a Grieving Wife by Helen Reichert Lambin. Forty-seven short, insightful reflections for a wife who has lost a husband. Deals with the anger, grief, and losses of widowhood, as well as the memories, hopes, and love. (128 pages, $8.95)

The Death of a Wife: Reflections for a Grieving Husband by Robert L. Vogt. A collection of poignant reflections for any husband mourning the death of his wife. Each of the thirty-one brief stories, remembrances, meditations, and poems considers a different facet of the grieving process. (112 pages, $8.95)

Always Precious in Our Memory: Reflections after Miscarriage, Stillbirth or Neonatal Death by Kristen Johnson Ingram. Here are short, heartfelt meditations combined with carefully chosen Scripture quotations that help parents, family members, and friends understand the grief, regret, anger, and guilt they may be feeling at the death of a baby. (94 pages, $8.95)

AVAILABLE FROM BOOKSELLERS OR CALL 800-397-2282